UNDERSTANDING CLIMATE

by Megan Cooley Peterson

PEBBLE
a capstone imprint

Pebble is published by Capstone,
1710 Roe Crest Drive, North Mankato, Minnesota 56003
www.capstonepub.com

Library of Congress Cataloging-in-Publication data is available on the Library of Congress website.
ISBN: 978-1-9771-3351-9 (library binding)
ISBN: 978-1-9771-3345-8 (paperback)
ISBN: 978-1-9771-5518-4 (eBook PDF)

Summary: Explains what climate is, including different types of climate, what causes climate, and the difference between weather and climate.

Editorial Credits
Editor: Mandy Robbins; Designer: Heidi Thompson; Media Researcher: Tracy Cummins; Production Specialist: Katy LaVigne

Photo Credits
Capstone Press: 11 bottom, 14, 19 top, 24; Getty Images: Brian Vander Brug, 5 bottom; iStockphoto: 4FR, 10; Shutterstock: Albert Beukhof, 25, Alex Tihonovs, 18, Color4260, design element, Creative Travel Projects, 21 bottom left, Dale Lorna Jacobsen, 15, Jacob Boomsma, 19 bottom, Jason Patrick Ross, cover, design element, 1, Jo Reason, 12, LeManna, 21 top left, LiliGraphie, 9, Michal Staniewski, 28, Nasky, 23, Polarer, 27, PVStocker, 5 top, S.Borisov, 21 top right, Samantha Crimmin, 22, Soleil Nordic, 8, Spotmatik Ltd, 29, Tibesty, 6, Toroslarinsesi, 21 bottom right, Traveller70, 16, Vaclav Sebek, 7, Vinnikava Viktoryia, 17, Volodymyr Burdiak, 11 top, worldswildlifewonders, 13

TABLE OF CONTENTS

Words in **bold** are in the glossary.

WHAT IS CLIMATE?

You and your family are going to a **tropical** beach. It is a warm, wet place all year. You pack T-shirts. You pack a swimsuit. You leave your snow boots behind.

Climate is the usual weather in a place. Scientists travel to different places. They record temperatures. They track snowfall and rainfall too. Scientists study places for at least 30 years. Then they give each place a climate name. These scientists study how climates change over time.

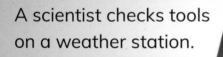
A scientist checks tools on a weather station.

Earth has four main climate **zones**. They are tropical, dry, **temperate**, and cold. Some zones overlap.

HOW PEOPLE CHANGE

Plants and animals are not the only living things that have ways to fit into their climate. Humans do too! We wear light or warm clothing. We heat and cool buildings. In rainy places, we carry umbrellas.

A polar bear's fur helps it survive in the cold climate.

Different kinds of plants and animals live in each zone. They have special ways to fit the climate. Animals in cold climates have thick fur. The fur keeps them warm. Many plants in **rain forests** have pointed tips. These drip tips help rain run off the leaves quickly.

THE SUN

What does the sun have to do with climate? A lot! The sun heats the ground and air. Places near the **equator** get stronger sunlight. The sun's rays don't have to travel as far. These places are hot. They can be dry or rainy.

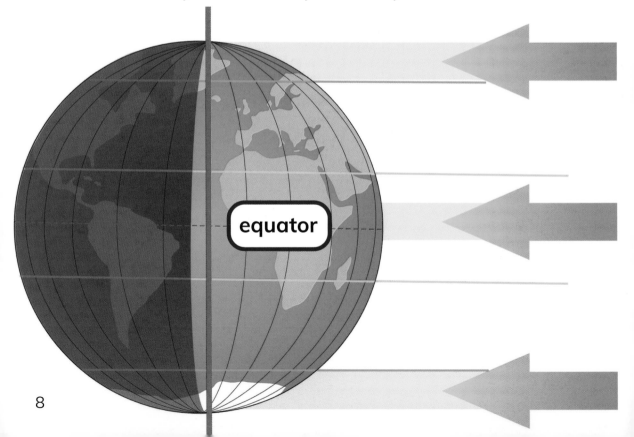

equator

Places north and south of the equator get weaker sunlight. The sun's rays must travel farther to reach them. The rays are also more spread out. These places usually have cooler climates.

Warm tropical islands are found near the equator.

TROPICAL CLIMATES

Warm tropical climates are near Earth's equator. Many of Earth's rainiest places are found here. Some places get a lot of rain all year. Others have wet and dry seasons.

Most tropical places are hot all year. But some places do get cold. Mountains there still get snow. Some islands are cold too. Cool ocean water makes them cold.

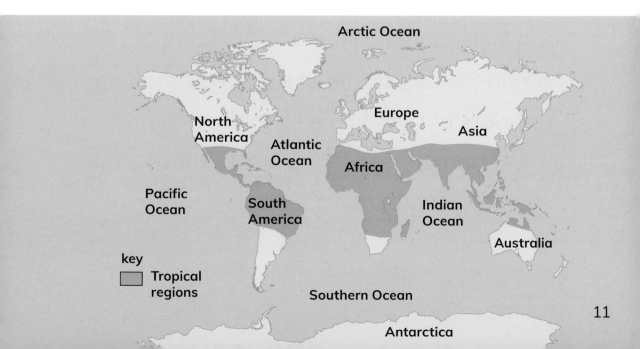

Arctic Ocean

North America

Atlantic Ocean

Europe

Asia

Africa

Pacific Ocean

South America

Indian Ocean

Australia

key

Tropical regions

Southern Ocean

Antarctica

11

African animals graze in a savanna.

Life in a Tropical Climate

Rain forests and **savannas** grow in tropical places. They are usually hot. A rain forest has lots of tall trees. It gets lots of rain. Some savannas have a wet and dry season. Grasses and shrubs grow there.

Many animals live in these places. In Africa, zebras and antelopes eat savanna grasses. Lions and cheetahs hunt them. In South America, spider monkeys hide in rain forest treetops. Big cats hunt them.

A spider monkey dangles from a tree.

DRY CLIMATES

Dry climates are found all around Earth. These **deserts** get little rain. Summers are usually very hot. Winters can be warm or cool during the day. At night, air gets colder.

Arctic Ocean

Europe

North America

Atlantic Ocean

Asia

Africa

Pacific Ocean

South America

Indian Ocean

Australia

key

Desert regions

Southern Ocean

Antarctica

Taylor Dry Valley, Antarctica

Not all dry places are warm. Some places in Antarctica are very dry. They have no ice or snow. They are also some of the coldest places on Earth.

Life in a Dry Climate

Deserts get less than 6 inches (15 centimeters) of rain each year. Sand and gravel cover the land. But plants still find ways to grow. Desert plants have thick stems and leaves. These parts hold in water. **Spines** keep away hungry animals.

Desert cactuses have sharp spines.

Animals in dry places also find ways to live. Camels can go weeks without water. Sometimes food is hard to find. They store fat in their humps. The fat gives them energy when food is hard to find. Many desert animals sleep during the day. They come out at night when it's cooler.

TEMPERATE CLIMATES

Temperate climates are between tropical and cold ones. In these places, temperatures are mild near oceans. Oceans don't warm or cool quickly. Neither do these areas. Summers aren't too hot. Winters usually aren't very cold. During winter, it often rains.

A seaport in Genoa Italy

Temperate climates far from oceans have different weather. Winters can be freezing cold. Lots of snow falls. Summers can be very hot. They can have strong storms.

Duluth, Minnesota, during winter

Life in a Temperate Climate

Temperate places have four seasons. They are summer, fall, winter, and spring. Summer is the warmest. Bees buzz. Flowers bloom. In fall, it gets cooler. Tree leaves turn colors. Then they drop to the ground. Winter is cold. Some animals **hibernate**. In some places, heavy snow falls. In spring, it gets warmer. Snow melts. Plants grow again, and animals wake up.

summer

fall

winter

spring

COLD CLIMATE ZONES

Most cold climates are found in Antarctica and the Arctic. They are also found high up in mountains. Temperatures can drop below -122 degrees Fahrenheit (-85 degrees Celsius). Many of these places have a lot of snow and ice. Others are very dry.

Penguins in Antarctica

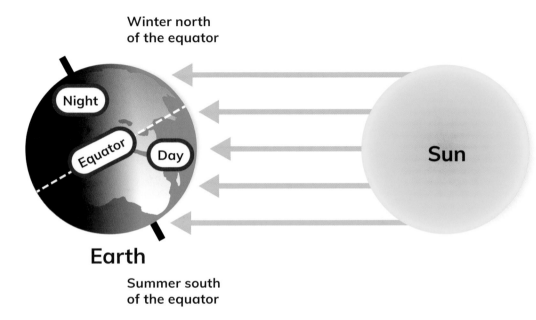

Winter north
of the equator

Night

Equator

Day

Sun

Earth

Summer south
of the equator

Some cold places go a long time without sunlight. The North and South Poles tilt away from the sun in winter. It is dark during the day. The sun doesn't rise for 11 weeks. When it is winter at one pole, it is summer at the other.

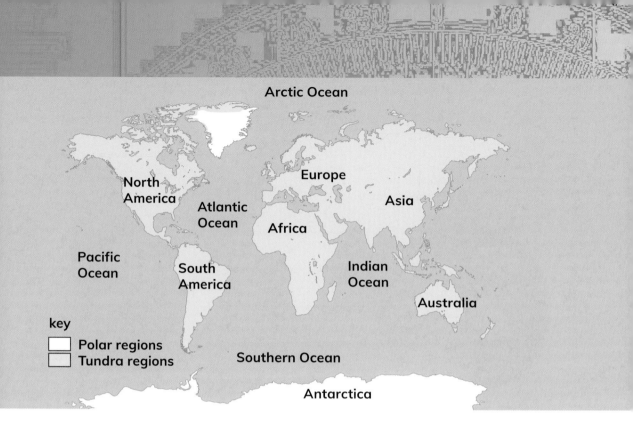

Arctic Ocean

North America

Europe

Asia

Atlantic Ocean

Africa

Pacific Ocean

South America

Indian Ocean

Australia

key

Polar regions
Tundra regions

Southern Ocean

Antarctica

Life in a Cold Climate

Tundras are in cold climates. Few people live there. The soil just below the surface is always frozen. It is called **permafrost**. Some plants do grow in tundras. In summer, shrubs, mosses, and **lichens** grow. They are low to the ground.

A brown bear walks through a taiga.

Taigas also grow in cold climates. They are large evergreen forests. Thick tree bark blocks out the cold.

ANIMALS IN COLD CLIMATES

Mammals in cold climates have thick fur. Polar bears also have a fat layer that keeps them warm. Arctic birds fly to warmer places in the winter. Other animals, such as brown bears, hibernate.

MOUNTAIN CLIMATES

Mountains make their own climate! Air gets colder higher up a mountain. Mountaintops have snow and wind. Not much grows there. Moving down a mountain, the air warms. Forests and grasslands grow there.

Mountains are very tall. Clouds bump into them! The side where the clouds are gets the most rain. The side without the clouds is very dry. It is called a rain shadow.

A mountain's climate changes the higher up it goes.

27

CLIMATE CHANGE

Climate change is a long-term change in weather patterns. Earth's climate has always changed. These changes usually take thousands of years. Scientists agree that Earth's climate is getting warmer. But it is changing faster than in the past.

Air pollution is making Earth's climate warmer.

Pollution from people is speeding up climate change. But we can work together to slow it down. We can do this by saving energy. Ride your bike instead of riding in a car. When you leave a room, turn off the lights.

GLOSSARY

desert (DE-zuhrt)—a dry area with little rain

equator (i-KWAY-tuhr)—an imaginary line around the middle of Earth

hibernate (HYE-bur-nate)—to spend winter in a deep sleep

lichen (LYE-ken)—a flat, mosslike plant that grows on trees and rocks

permafrost (PUR-muh-frawst)—a layer of frozen earth underground that never thaws, even in summer

pollution (puh-LOO-shuhn)—materials that hurt Earth's water, air, and land

rain forest (RAYN FOR-ist)—a thick forest or jungle where at least 100 inches (254 centimeters) of rain falls every year

savanna (suh-VAN-uh)—a flat, grassy area with few trees

spine (SPINE)—a hard, sharp, pointed growth such as a thorn or cactus needle

taiga (TYE-guh)—a forest with mainly pine trees

temperate (TEM-pur-uht)—not too hot, cold, or wet; places between the polar zones and tropical zones are temperate

tropical (TRAH-pih-kuhl)—of or near the equator; in weather, hot and humid

tundra (TUHN-druh)—a cold area where trees do not grow

zone (ZOHN)—an area that is separate from other areas